Big Book of
Playtime Activities

Ray Gibson

Designed by Amanda Barlow
Edited by Fiona Watt and Jenny Tyler
Illustrated by Amanda Barlow and Michaela Kennard
Photography by Howard Allman and Ray Moller

Contents

I can cut and stick 1
I can crayon 33
I can fingerpaint 65
I can draw animals 97
I can count 129
I can add up 161
Fun with numbers 193

I can cut and stick

A truck	2
A caterpillar	4
Flowers and bees	6
A snake card	8
A crown	10
A hanging fish	12
A bonfire	14
A spoon princess	16
An octopus puppet	18
A big bug	20
A snow picture	22
A pecking bird	24
A necklace	26
A firework	28
A big-nosed clown	30
A brooch	32

A truck

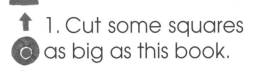

1. Cut some squares as big as this book.

2. Fold one in half and in half again. Cut along the folds.

Stick on a window

3. Stick down two big squares and one small one.

Decorate with strips of paper. Stick on letters from magazines.

4. Cut some wheels from dark paper.

5. Stick them on. Add foil hub caps.

A caterpillar

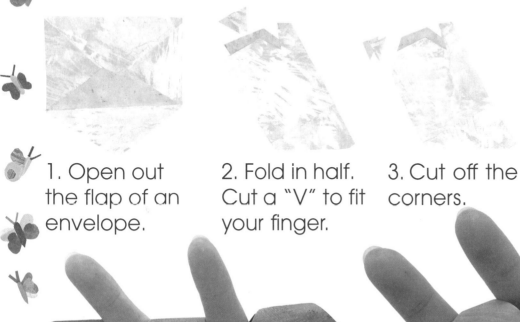

1. Open out the flap of an envelope.

2. Fold in half. Cut a "V" to fit your finger.

3. Cut off the corners.

4. Open out. Sponge paint on both sides.

4

5. Cut eyes and a big smile from paper. Stick them on.

Stick fingers through holes.

Flowers and bees

1. Draw a flower with a wax crayon.

2. Cut it out. Stick on a paper middle.

3. Make some more flowers and leaves.

4. Draw bees. Crayon eyes and stripes. Cut bees out.

Stick the wings on the bees.

5. Draw wings. Cut them out.

6. Stick everything down in a pattern.

7

A snake card

1. Fold a long piece of cardboard in half.

2. Cut a long strip of gift wrap. Fold in half.

3. Fold in half again. Then open out.

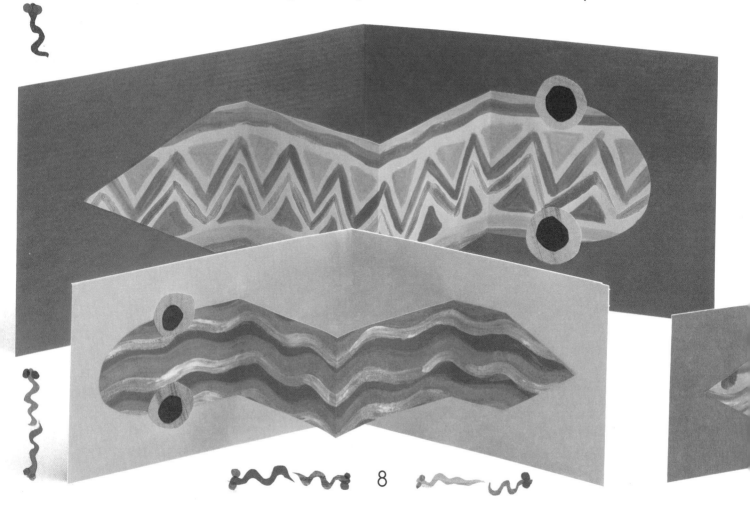

8

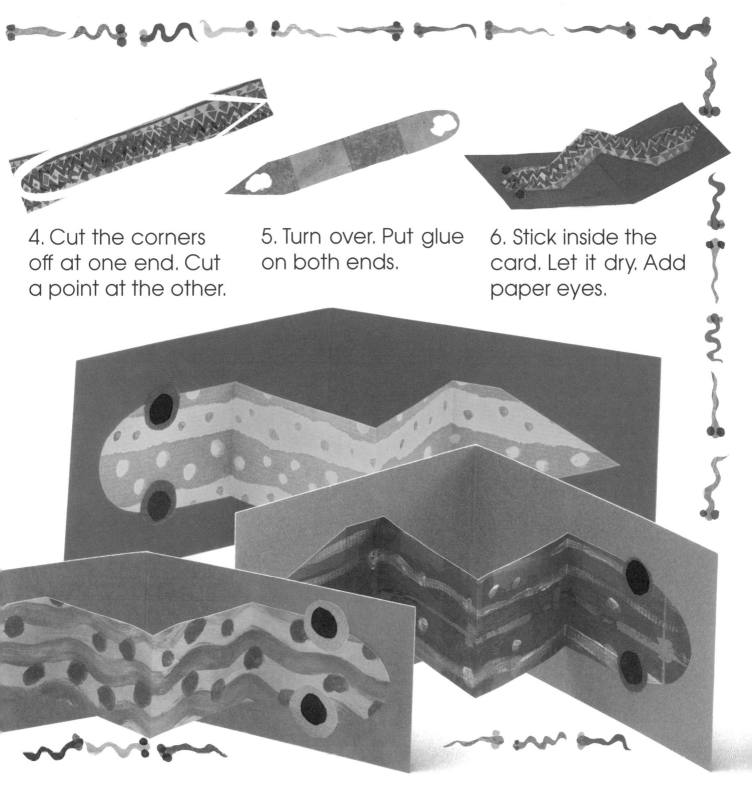

4. Cut the corners off at one end. Cut a point at the other.

5. Turn over. Put glue on both ends.

6. Stick inside the card. Let it dry. Add paper eyes.

A crown

1. Fold a gold or silver doily in half.

2. Cut a strip of folded foil to fit around your head.

3. Put the folded foil inside the doily.

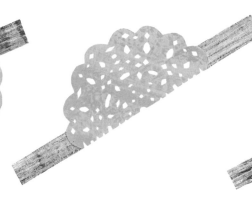

4. Open the doily. Put glue all around the bottom edge.

5. Fold it again, with the foil inside, so the sides stick.

6. Stick on scraps of shiny paper, ribbon, and crumpled tissue.

Tape the crown to fit your head

If you don't have a gold or silver doily, dab paint on a white one.

A hanging fish

1. Draw a fish shape on bright paper.

2. Cut it out. Glue on an eye.

3. Cut some strips. Glue them on.

Tape on a string to hang your fish up.

4. Stick on some shapes. Cut off what you don't need.

5. Cut some paper spikes. Glue them at the top.

6. Cut long pieces of tissue paper for a tail. Stick them on.

13

A bonfire

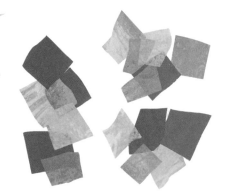

1. Cut red, orange and yellow shapes from magazines or giftwrap.

2. Cut into flame shapes. Make the ends pointed.

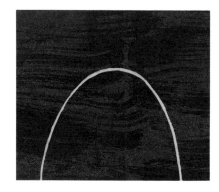

3. Draw a tall shape like a hill on dark paper.

4. Stick yellow flames at the top, orange flames below, then red.

5. Fill the spaces with leftover flames. Add black sticks. Cross them over.

6. Use wisps of cotton ball for smoke, and kitchen foil pieces and stars for sparks.

A spoon princess

1. Paint the back of a wooden spoon.

2. Cut cloth as wide as this book and as tall as your spoon.

3. Wrap it around the spoon. Tape at the top.

4. Fasten it on with a rubber band.

You could stick on sequins.

5. Tape knitting yarn to the back, then sides of the head.

6. Cut out and stick on a paper crown. Draw on a face.

An octopus puppet

1. Cut a paper plate like this. You need both pieces.

2. Turn the big piece over. Use a sponge to wipe green paint all over.

3. Wipe green paint on both sides of a sheet of strong paper. Roll it up.

4. Cut the roll into pieces, like this. Then unroll them.

5. Stick them to the unpainted side of the plate.

6. Tape the small piece of plate to the back, for a handle.

Stick on paper eyes and a mouth.

You can add some patterns to your octopus.

A big bug

Paint these too.

1. Cut a cardboard egg carton in two. Paint both pieces.

2. Cut the round parts from another carton, for feet.

3. Cut three pipe-cleaners in half. Stick them to the feet.

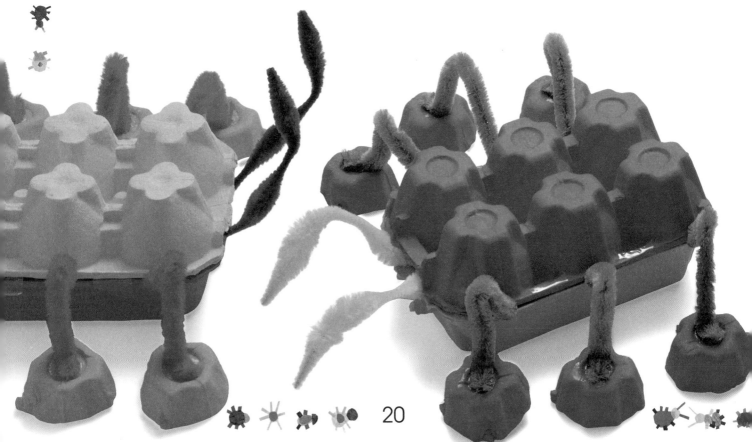

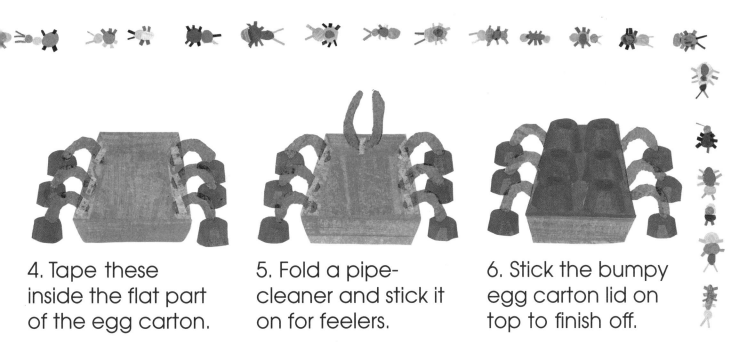

4. Tape these inside the flat part of the egg carton.

5. Fold a pipe-cleaner and stick it on for feelers.

6. Stick the bumpy egg carton lid on top to finish off.

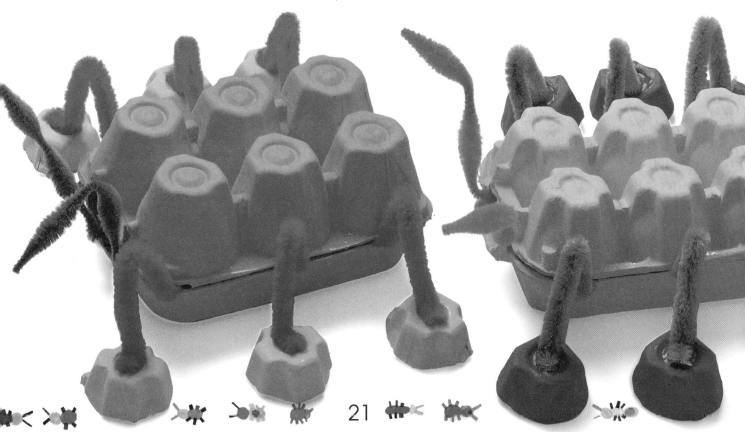

A snow picture

1. Cut a cardboard circle. Paint it blue.

2. Cut tree parts from brown paper. Stick them on.

3. Cut green cloth or paper. Stick on for bushes.

4. Stick on pieces of cotton ball for snow and a snowman.

5. Add a hat, scarf and face cut from paper or cloth.

6. Stick on a kitchen foil moon, and some icicles on the tree.

Tape on a loop
for hanging.

23

A pecking bird

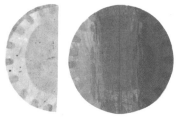   

1. Fold a paper plate. Unfold. Paint stripes on the back.

2. Fold it again. Stick a paper beak inside.

3. Cut some paper into spikes.

4. Stick them on the head. Add an eye.

Cut feather shapes and stick them on if you like.

5. Cut strips of bright tissue as long as your hand.

6. Twist them together. Tape them at the back for a tail.

Rock your bird to make it peck.

A necklace

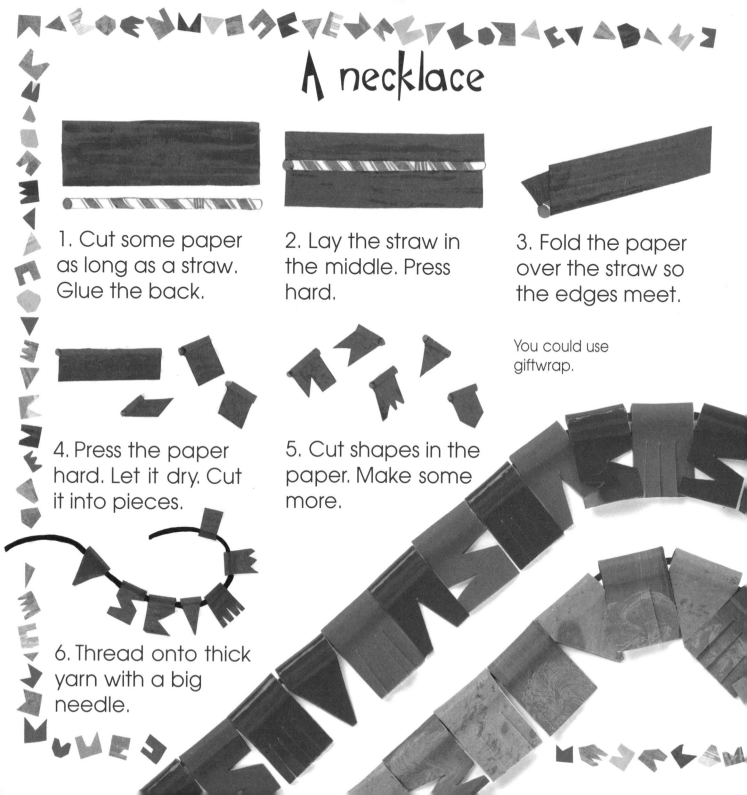

1. Cut some paper as long as a straw. Glue the back.

2. Lay the straw in the middle. Press hard.

3. Fold the paper over the straw so the edges meet.

You could use giftwrap.

4. Press the paper hard. Let it dry. Cut it into pieces.

5. Cut shapes in the paper. Make some more.

6. Thread onto thick yarn with a big needle.

Tie the ends to fit around your neck or wrist.

A firework

1. Stick bands of paper around a toilet roll.

2. Add some sticky shapes.

3. Stick red and yellow paper onto kitchen foil. Let it dry.

4. Cut this paper into thin pieces.

5. Stick the strips inside the top.

Use a kitchen paper towel roll for a big firework.

29

A big-nosed clown

1. Poke a hole in a paper plate with a pencil.

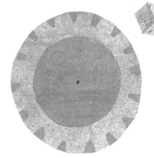

2. Wipe the back all over with bright paint. Let it dry.

3. Stick on two buttons for eyes, and a paper mouth.

4. Cut up some bright yarn and glue it on for hair.

5. Cut shapes for a hat from cardboard or a box.

6. Stick on a flower from a magazine or seed packet.

7. Get help to blow up a balloon a little way.

8. Poke it through the hole. Tape it at the back.

His nose will
wobble if you
shake his head.

31

A brooch

1. Draw a pig like this on stiff paper.

2. Cut it out. Stick on a button nose.

3. Tape a safety pin on the back.

You could make a fish...

...or a cat...

...or a flower.

32

I can crayon

Little fat birds	34	A fishy scene	50
Spiders in the dark	36	Decorations	52
A big crane	38	A caterpillar	54
A duck card	40	A piggy puppet	56
A flower picture	42	Big trucks	58
Fireworks	44	Decorated eggs	60
A tall giraffe	46	A butterfly	62
Loopy snakes	48	Lots of shapes	64

Little fat birds

1. Crayon a fat body.

2. Fill in the shape. Add a beak.

3. Draw an eye near the beak. Add a wing.

This bird is feeding a worm to her baby.

4. Crayon a tail.
Give your bird some
legs.

This bird
has spiky
feathers
on its head.

Point the
wings up
for a flying
bird.

Spiders in the dark

1. Crayon a fat body.

2. Add big eyes.

3. Crayon in the body.

4. Draw 8 legs,
and a thread
to hang from.

5. Crayon some
more spiders.

6. Cover with
runny paint.

A big crane

1. Crayon the cab. Leave a window hole.

2. Crayon the lifting part.

3. Draw the cable.

You could add some stripes.

4. Crayon some wheels.

5. Draw what the crane is lifting.

Draw some people.

This crane is lifting a car.

A duck card

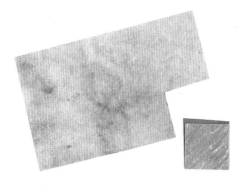

1. Cut off the corner of an envelope. Crayon the inside. Crayon the top.

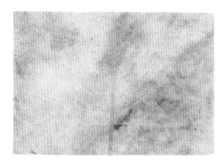

2. Fold paper to make a card. Open it up again.

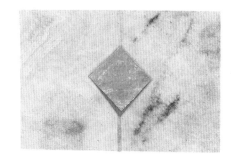

3. Glue the envelope corner in the middle. This makes a beak.

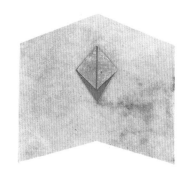

4. Lift the top up with a finger. Close the card. Squash flat.

5. Open it up. Draw a duck's head around the beak. Draw some eyes.

6. Crayon flowers and leaves around your duck.

A flower picture

1. Cut a round shape from an old birthday card.

2. Glue it onto some paper.

3. Cut out petals. Glue them on.

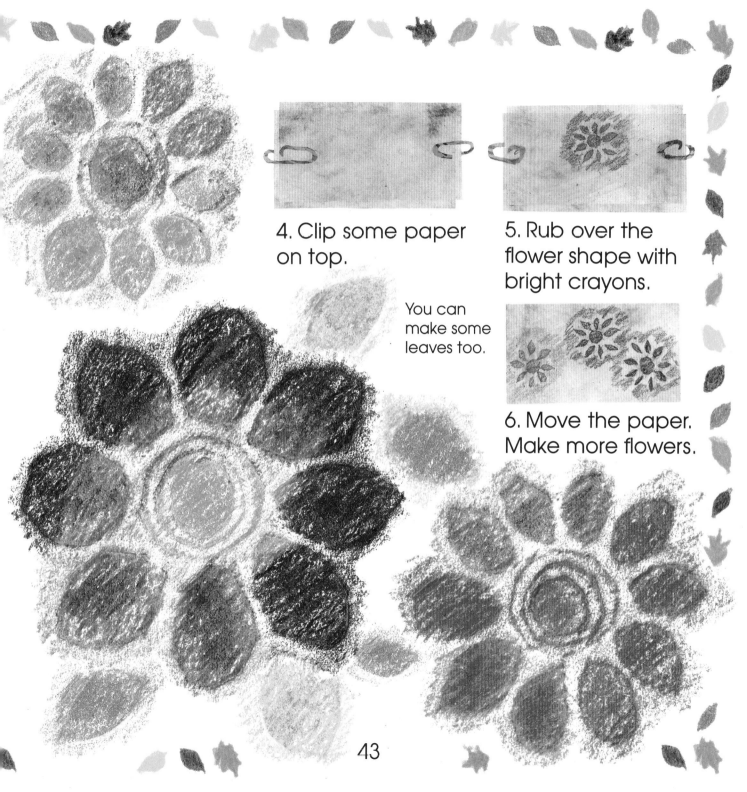

4. Clip some paper on top.

5. Rub over the flower shape with bright crayons.

You can make some leaves too.

6. Move the paper. Make more flowers.

43

Fireworks

1. Crayon a big firework. Press hard.

2. Add lots of sparks and squiggles.

3. Paint all over with runny dark paint.

A tall giraffe

1. Crayon a yellow body.

2. Draw a long neck.

3. Crayon the head.

4. Draw long thin legs with brown feet.

Draw some leaves and flowers.

5. Add an ear and two horns.

6. Put in an eye. Add a tail, and patches.

Loopy snakes

1. Crayon patterns and stripes all over strong thin paper.

2. Cut the paper into strips - some fat, some thin.

3. Cut a thin point for a head. Cut a fat point for a tail.

You can overlap the snakes when you stick them down.

48

4. Put glue under the head and tail.

5. Bend and stick onto paper.

6. Stick on eyes made from circles cut in half.

49

A fishy scene

1. Fold thin strong paper.

2. Open it out and crayon thickly over one half.

3. Fold again. Draw a big fish with patterns, using a hard pencil.

Make
lots of
fish.

Draw some
shells too.

4. Open the paper.
Cut your fish out and
glue onto paper.

Crayon a sea
background.

Decorations

You could use a paper square

1. Crayon over a paper circle.

2. Fold it in half, and then in half again.

3. Cut shapes in the edges.

4. Open it out.

A caterpillar

1. Put a fat crayon on your paper, like this.

2. Push it up and down across the paper for a body.

3. Draw a head.

4. Add some eyes and a mouth.

5. Give him lots of feet, and a tail.

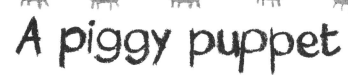

A piggy puppet

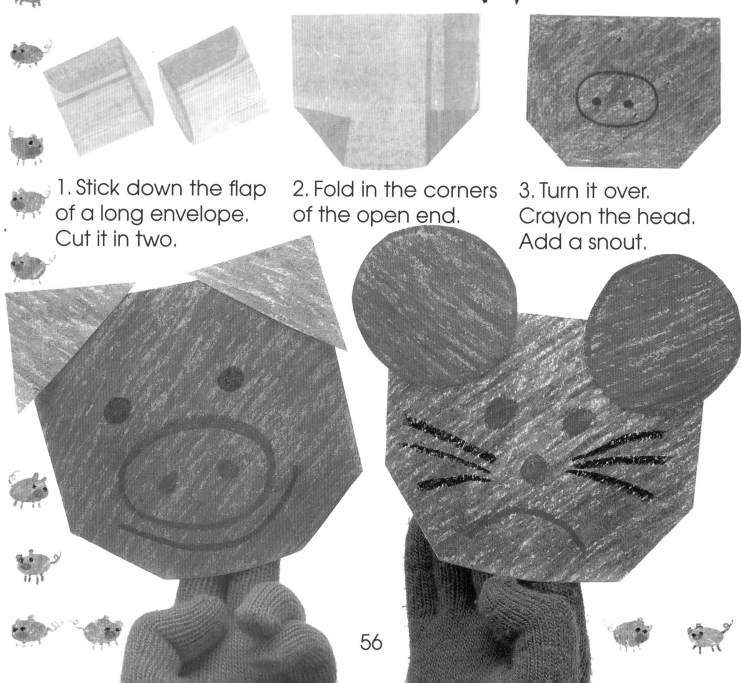

1. Stick down the flap of a long envelope. Cut it in two.

2. Fold in the corners of the open end.

3. Turn it over. Crayon the head. Add a snout.

4. Draw two eyes, and a mouth.

Add big round ears for a mouse.

5. Cut the corners from the closed end of the other piece.

6. Crayon them. Glue them on.

Add big eyes for a frog.

Big trucks

1. Find an envelope or cut a rectangle.

2. Crayon patterns all over.

3. Paint with runny paint. Let it dry.

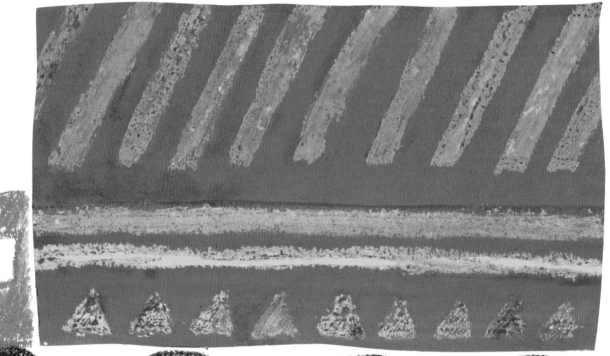

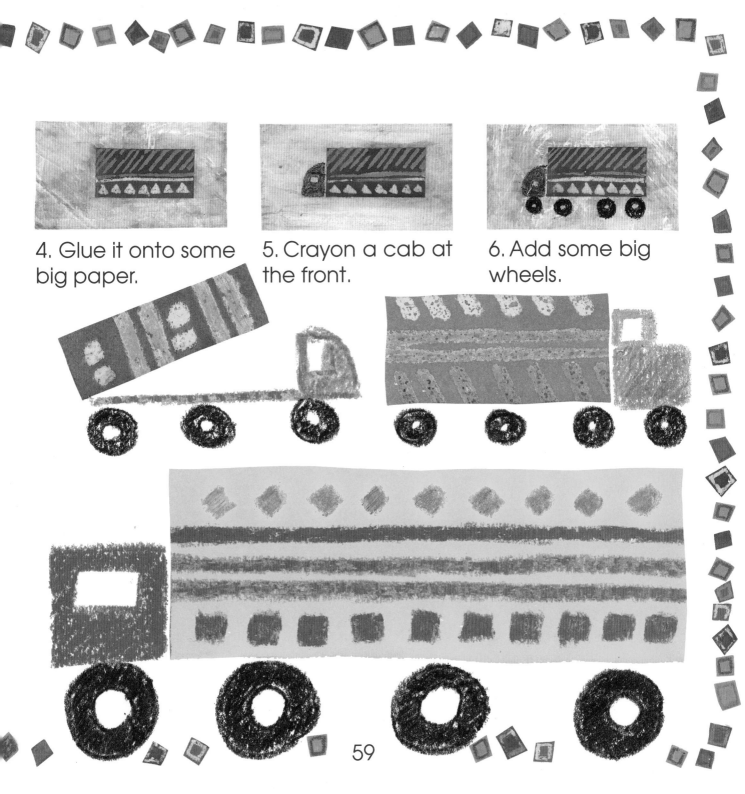

4. Glue it onto some big paper.

5. Crayon a cab at the front.

6. Add some big wheels.

59

Decorated eggs

1. Hard boil an egg. Crayon patterns on it.

2. Put some drops of food dye in a small bowl.

3. Put the egg in. Dab the dye all over with a paintbrush.

4. Lift it out with a spoon. Put it on paper towel to dry.

You can eat your egg if you like.

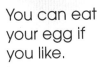

5. Put some cooking oil in a saucer.

6. Dip paper towel in the oil. Rub over the egg to make it shine.

A butterfly

1. Fold a piece of strong thin paper. Open it out.

2. Cut a card into pieces. Glue close together on one side.

3. Fold the paper again. Crayon over the top.

4. Cut the crayoned part off. Fold it. Draw two butterfly wings.

5. Cut out the wings. Open them out.

6. Crayon feelers and a body. Cut out and glue on.

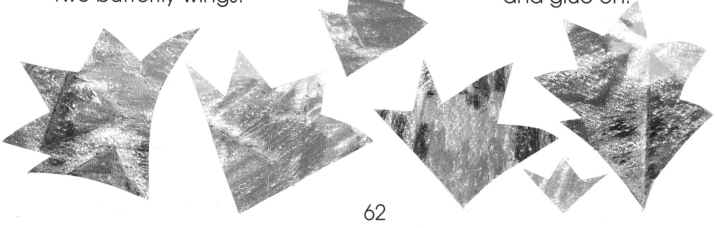

Make some
leaves from
the leftovers,
or crayon
some more.

63

Lots of shapes

1. Ask a grown-up to press the sharp side of a cookie cutter into half a potato.

2. Pour some paint on an old cloth or newspaper.

3. Press the cutter in the paint and then onto some paper.

4. Make more shapes. Let them dry. Crayon them.

I can finger paint

Spotty spiders	66	Lots of shapes	82
Cats	68	Snails in a puddle	84
Rainbow fish	70	An iceberg picture	86
A folding pattern	72	An angel	88
A rocket	74	An alligator	90
Lots of flowers	76	Spiky animals	92
An owl in a tree	78	A jungle picture	94
A field of rabbits	80	Funny creatures	96

Spotty spiders

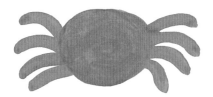

1. Dip your finger in paint. Go around and around to make a body.

2. Draw 8 legs with a fingertip dipped in paint.

3. Do some big white eyes. Put a dark dot in each one.

You can mix your paint with flour to make it thicker and dry quicker.

4. Dab bright spots
all over.

67

Cats

1. Go around and around with a painty finger for a body.

2. Add a smaller head.

3. Do the ears and tail with a fingertip.

4. Add whiskers. Do eyes and nose with a fingertip.

5. Dab white paint on the cheeks, chest and feet.

68

69

Rainbow fish

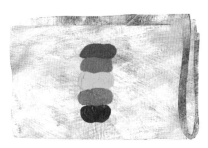

1. Spoon different paints close together on newspaper.

2. Press your hand on the paint and then on the paper.

3. Turn the shape around. Paint a tail with your finger.

4. Add an eye, and bright spots.

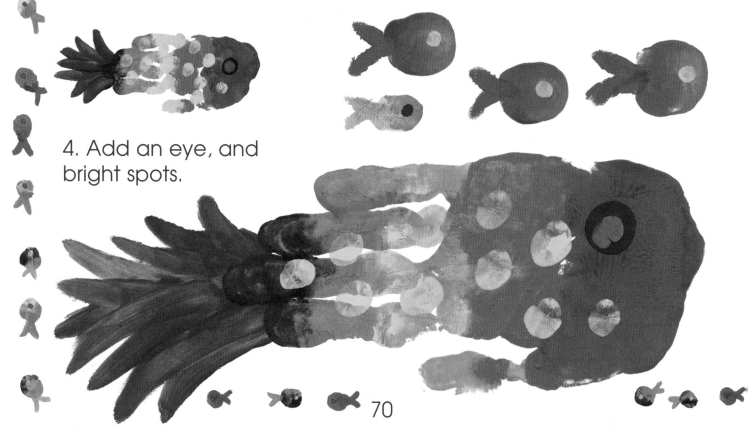

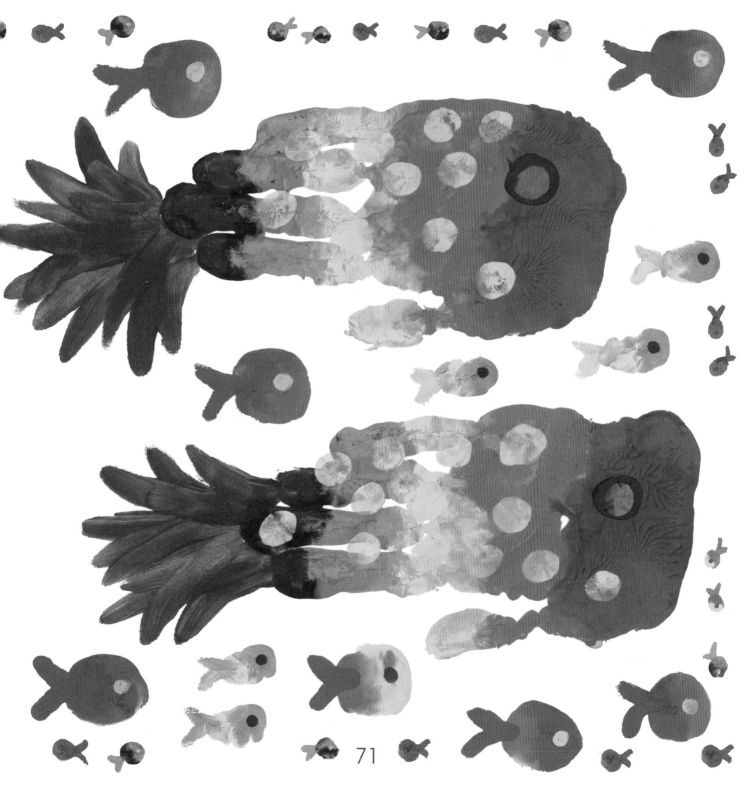

A folding pattern

1. Fold some paper. Open out. Press your hand in paint.

2. Press your hand on one side of the paper.

3. Wash your hands. Fold the paper. Press it all over.

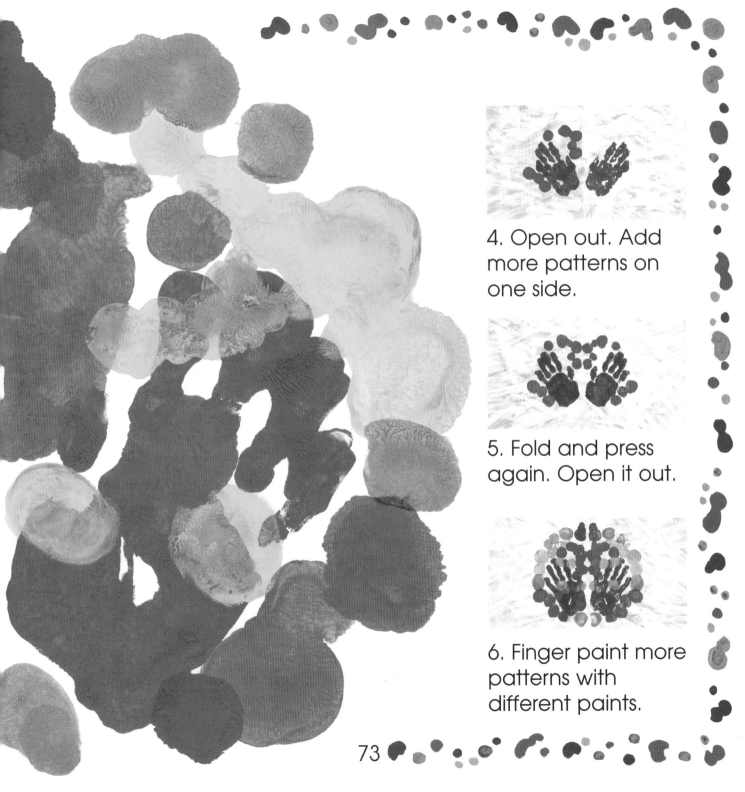

4. Open out. Add more patterns on one side.

5. Fold and press again. Open it out.

6. Finger paint more patterns with different paints.

73

A rocket

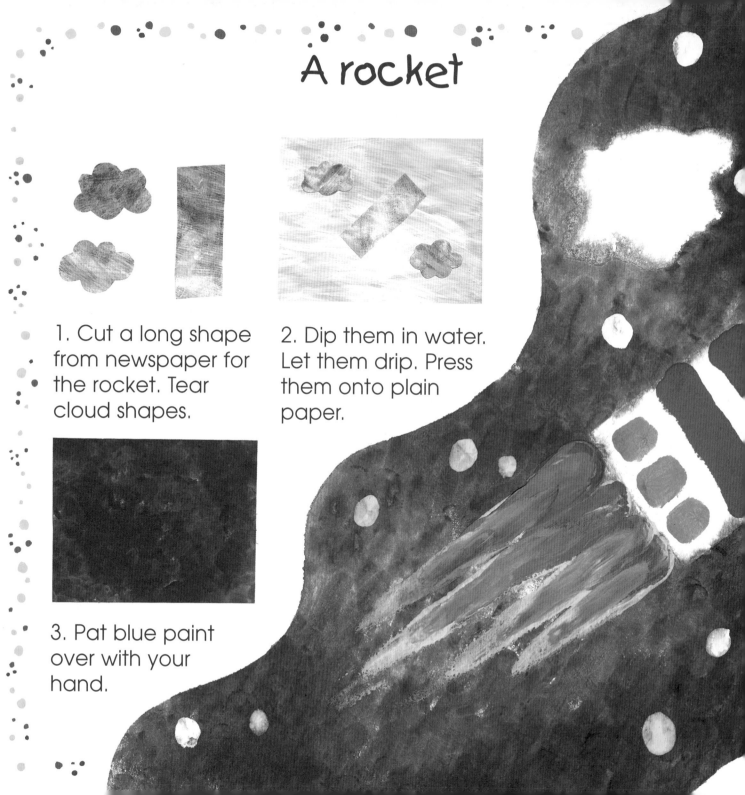

1. Cut a long shape from newspaper for the rocket. Tear cloud shapes.

2. Dip them in water. Let them drip. Press them onto plain paper.

3. Pat blue paint over with your hand.

4. Peel off the newspaper shapes. Let it dry.

5. Paint the rocket's nose with a finger. Add patterns and yellow flames.

6. Do red flames on top of the yellow ones. Add stars with a fingertip.

75

Lots of flowers

1. Dip your finger in purple paint.

2. Make blue dots around the purple one.

1. Press two fingers in different paints. Go around and around.

2. Add green leaves with a finger.

1. Make a print with your thumb.

2. Make more prints underneath. Add a green stem.

An owl in a tree

1. Wet some paper with your hand. Rub yellow, orange and red paint on, like this.

2. Dip your finger in black paint. Use it to paint a tree trunk.

3. Add some long branches, using more black paint.

4. Do small branches and a hedge along the bottom.

5. Do an owl in the tree. Give him big eyes.

6. Paint a moon with your finger. Dot on some stars.

Field of rabbits

1. Press yellow handprints all over your paper. Add green handprints.

2. Finger paint a fat sausage on top for a rabbit's body.

3. Add the head.

Dab on
flowers with
a fingertip

4. Finger paint ears
and legs.

5. Do a white tail.

Lots of shapes

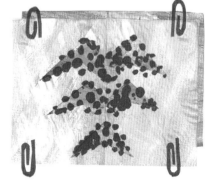

1. Fold a piece of paper in half. Cut some shapes out of the folded side.

2. Open it out. Paper clip it onto another piece of paper.

3. Dot paint over the shapes with your fingertip.

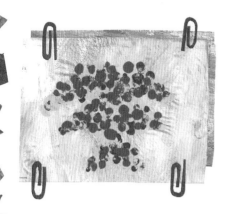

4. Dot more paint on top so the shapes are covered.

5. Lift off the top sheet to see the pattern.

83

Snails in a puddle

1. Wet some paper with your hand. Dip your fingers in paint. Make watery patterns. Let them dry.

2. Use different paper. Make a green circle with your finger.

3. Go around and around on the green with a darker green finger.

4. Add a body and horns. Let it dry. Cut out and stick onto the puddle.

85

An iceberg picture

1. Tear an iceberg shape from the edge of newspaper. Wet it.

2. Lay it on paper, like this. Add more shapes.

3. Dip your hands in blue paint. Pat them all over.

4. Add some green, then a little white.

5. Peel off the shapes carefully to see the icebergs.

6. Paint a canoe with a finger. Add some fishermen.

87

An angel

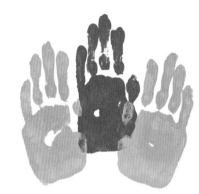

1. Make a whole handprint in the middle. This is an upside-down dress.

2. Make two whole hand prints a bit lower, for the wings.

3. Turn your paper. Go around and around with your finger for a head.

4. Use your fingertip to do arms and hands.

5. Finger paint some hair and a halo.

6. Dot on some eyes, and a nose. Paint a smiling mouth.

An alligator

1. Make a green print with the front of your fist.

2. Make more prints underneath.

3. Turn them this way. Paint the jaws with your finger.

90

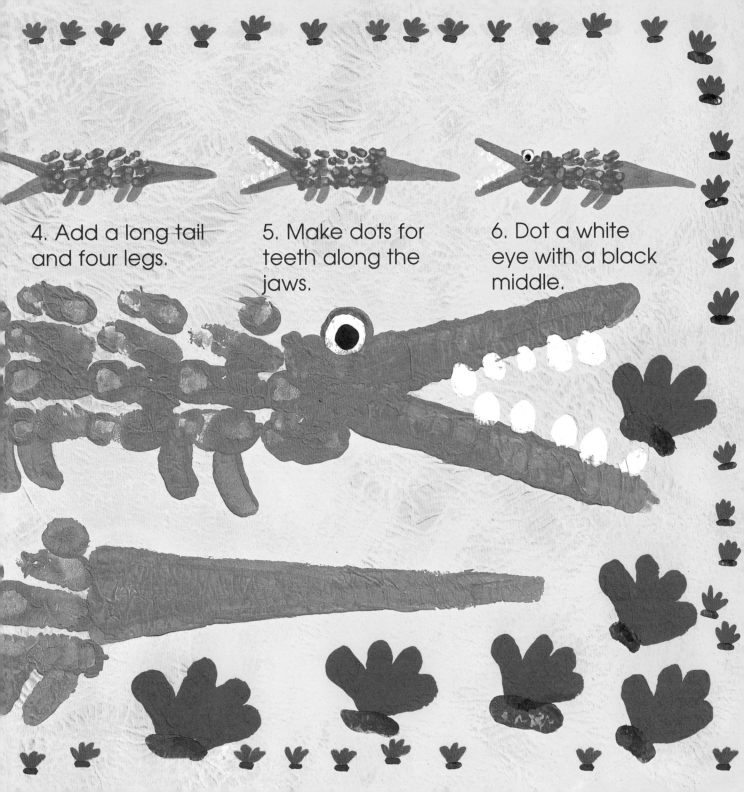

4. Add a long tail and four legs.

5. Make dots for teeth along the jaws.

6. Dot a white eye with a black middle.

Spiky animals

1. Dip your fingertip in paint. Go around and around for a body.

2. Make one end pointed for a snout.

3. Add an eye and a nose with your fingertip.

4. Finger paint spikes all over his back.

93

A jungle picture

1. Wet a large piece of paper. Let it drip.

2. Finger paint a green dot. Add leaves around it.

3. Do more of these in dark and light green. Leave to dry.

4. Paint a bird body with a finger. Add wings.

5. Dot a beak, the ends of the wings and tail. Add an eye.

6. Use your finger to dot on jungle flowers.

Funny creatures

1. Go around and around with a finger dipped in paint to make a blob.

2. Do spikes all around with different paint.

3. Add eyes, legs and feet with a fingertip.

I can draw animals

a lion	98	a fish	114
a cat	100	a monkey	116
a dolphin	102	a frog	118
a lizard	104	a horse	120
a rabbit	106	a turtle	122
a hen	108	a flamingo	124
a teddy	110	a reindeer	126
a tiger	112	a bee	128

a lion

1. Crayon the head.

2. Add two ears. Fill in with a felt pen.

3. Crayon a nose.

4. Add the mouth and two eyes.

5. Crayon a big bushy mane all around.

6. Add whiskers.

a cat

1. Crayon a round head.

2. Crayon a fat body.

3. Add two eyes and ears.

4. Crayon the nose and mouth.

The crayon will show through.

5. Add some whiskers, and a tail.

6. Crayon stripes. Go all over with a felt pen.

101

a dolphin

1. Crayon a curvy line for the tummy.

2. Crayon another curve for the back.

3. Add a long nose.

4. Crayon a fin on
top and underneath.

5. Draw in an eye.
Add the mouth.

6. Crayon the tail.
Fill in with a felt pen.

103

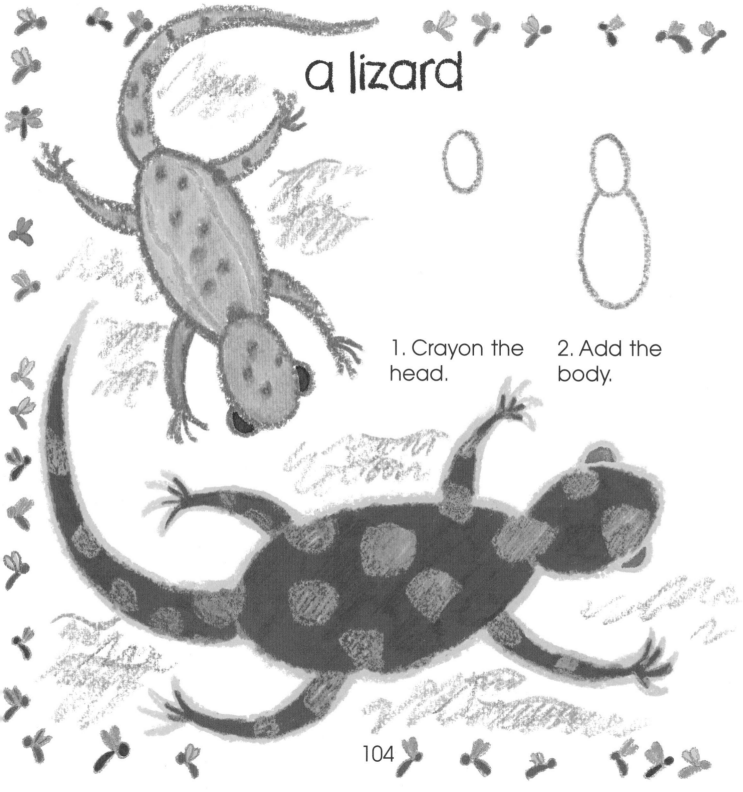

a lizard

1. Crayon the head.

2. Add the body.

104

3. Add the
legs and eyes.

4. Add a tail
and patterns.

5. Add toes.
Go over with
a felt pen.

a rabbit

1. Draw a round head.

2. Add two long ears.

3. Add the body.

4. Put in eyes and a nose.

5. Draw the mouth and tail.

6. Add whiskers. Fill in with a felt pen.

Draw some lettuces like this.

107

a hen

1. Crayon a body.

2. Add the neck and head part.

3. Add a beak and eye. Crayon a tail.

4. Do striped legs. Crayon wing feathers.

108

5. Crayon the red parts. Go over your hen with a felt pen.

Draw some chicks like this.

a teddy

1. Crayon a head.

2. Add ears and a muzzle.

3. Put in the eyes, nose and mouth.

4. Crayon a fat body.

5. Add the arms.

6. Draw the legs. Fill in with a felt pen.

111

a tiger

1. Draw a face. Fill it in with a felt pen.

2. Put in the eyes, nose and ears.

3. Add fur around the face.

4. Crayon a long shape for a body.

5. Draw the legs and the tail. Fill in with a felt pen.

6. Crayon black stripes. Add claws and whiskers.

Draw some
flowers and
creepers like
these.

113

a fish

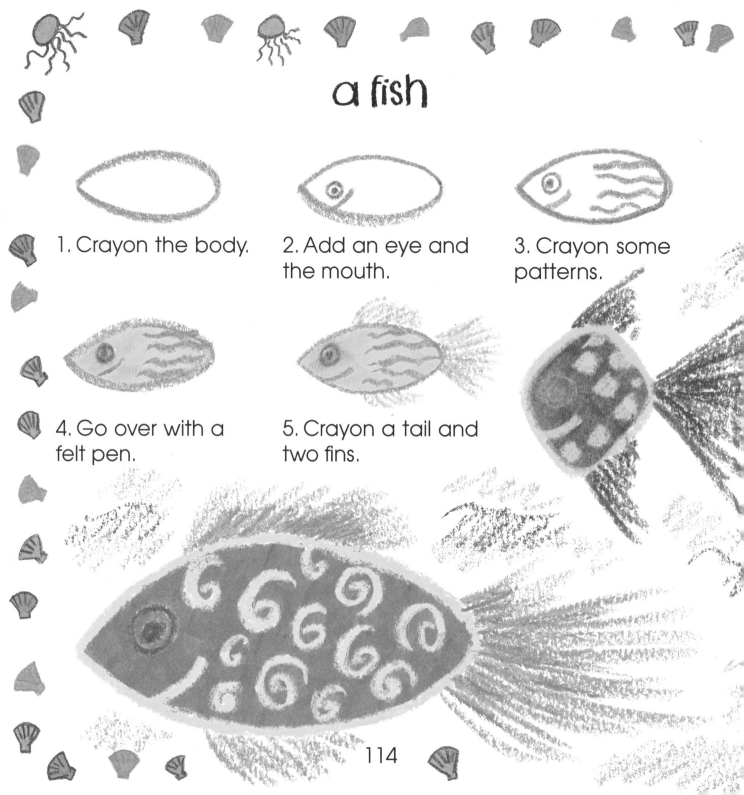

1. Crayon the body.

2. Add an eye and the mouth.

3. Crayon some patterns.

4. Go over with a felt pen.

5. Crayon a tail and two fins.

114

a monkey

1. Draw the head.

2. Add the body and a curly tail.

3. Add the muzzle and two ears.

4. Put in the eyes, nose and mouth.

116

5. Do the arms and legs.

6. Add hands and feet. Fill in with a felt pen.

117

a frog

1. Crayon a body.

2. Add big eyes, a mouth and nose.

3. Crayon the front legs. Add toes.

4. Crayon the back legs. Add toes.

5. Crayon spots. Go over with a felt pen.

Draw leaping
frogs like this.

a horse

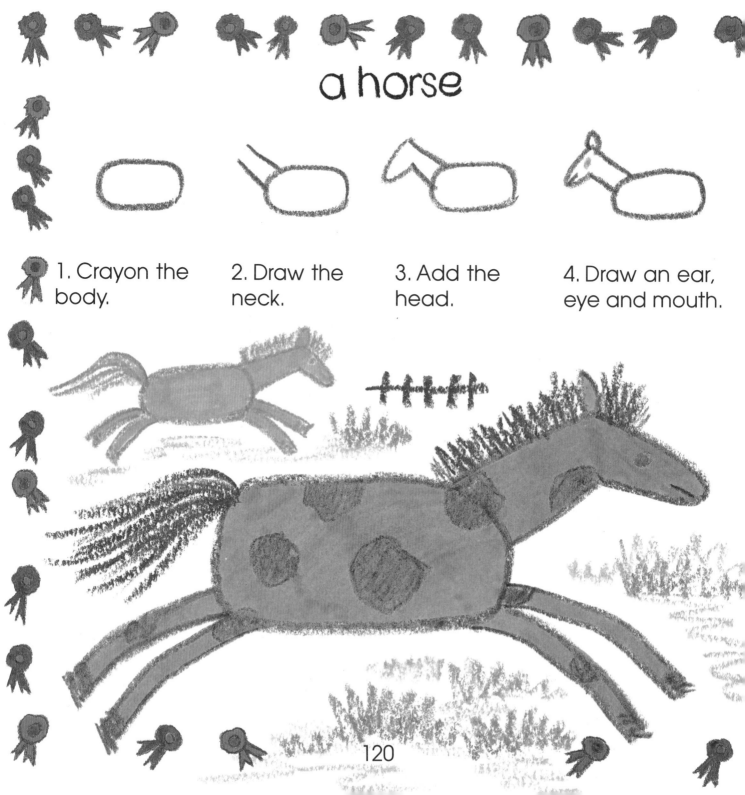

1. Crayon the body.

2. Draw the neck.

3. Add the head.

4. Draw an ear, eye and mouth.

120

5. Crayon four legs. Add the hooves.

6. Add a mane and tail. Fill in with a felt pen.

121

a turtle

1. Crayon a big, round shell.

2. Add the head. Put in the eyes and mouth.

3. Draw the front and back legs.

4. Add a tail. Crayon a pattern around the shell.

5. Crayon more patterns. Go over with a felt pen.

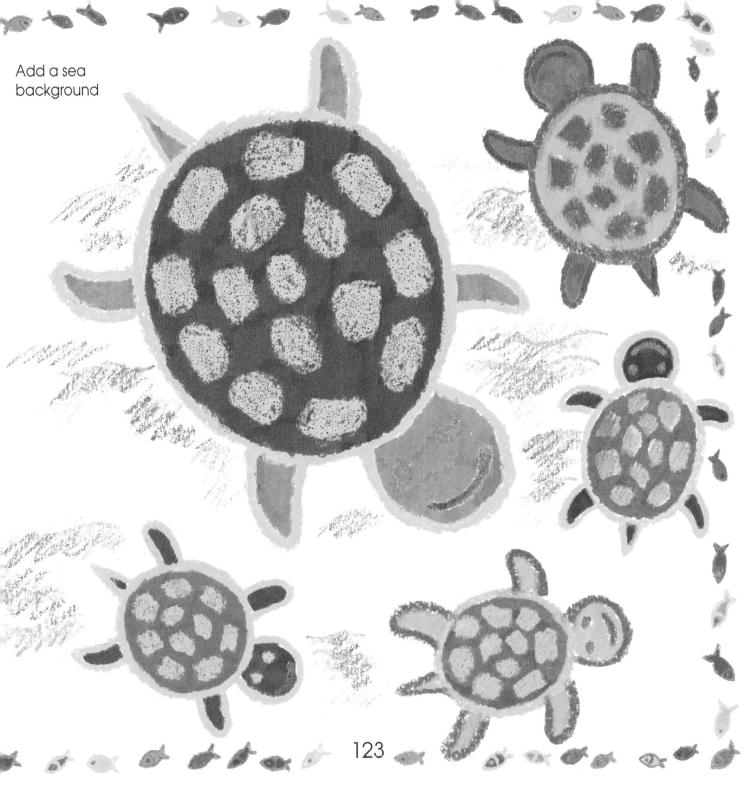

Add a sea
background

123

a flamingo

1. Crayon the body.

2. Add tail feathers and a neck.

3. Draw the head. Fill in with a felt pen.

4. Add a beak, an eye and feathers.

5. Draw long thin legs with knobbly knees.

6. Add the feet.

You could draw
your flamingo
standing in water.

a reindeer

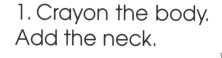

1. Crayon the body. Add the neck.

2. Do the head. Add two ears.

3. Add four long legs and a tail.

4. Crayon hooves, a nose and two eyes.

5. Draw jagged antlers.

6. Add spikes to them. Fill in with a felt pen.

a bee

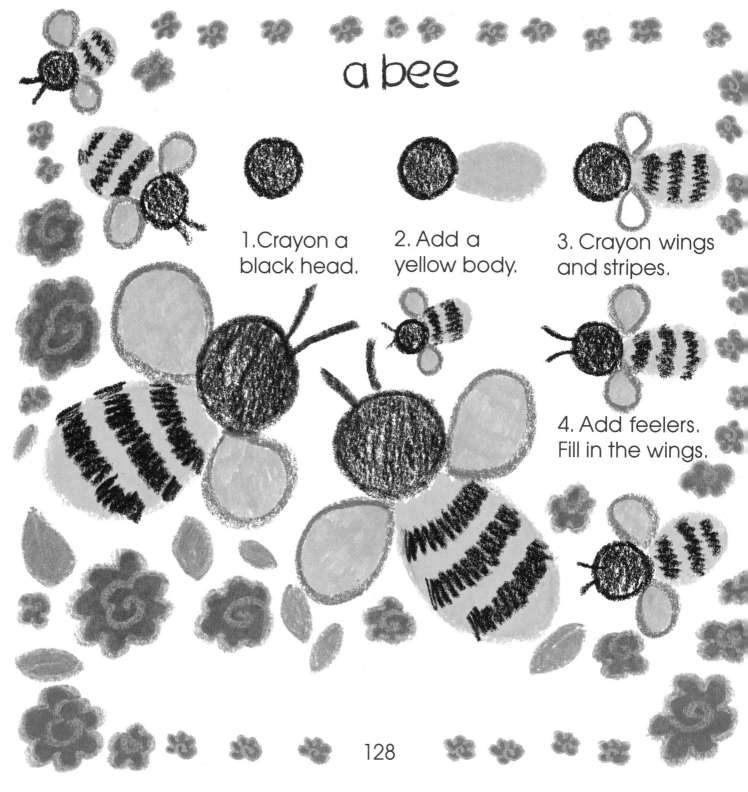

1. Crayon a black head.

2. Add a yellow body.

3. Crayon wings and stripes.

4. Add feelers. Fill in the wings.

I can count

I can count	130	I can count to 8	146
I can count to 1	132	I can count to 9	148
I can count to 2	134	I can count to 10	150
I can count to 3	136	I can count to 20	152
I can count to 4	138	I can count to 30	154
I can count to 5	140	I can count to 40	156
I can count to 6	142	I can count to 50	158
I can count to 7	144	Duck, fish and spider	160

I can count

Follow the instructions in this part of the book to print fun pictures, each based on a different number. Most of the printing is done with potatoes cut in half and your fingers. You will need a paintbrush to finish off some of the pictures.

Perhaps you can think of other things to print or paint for each number too.

Opposite you can see some tips on potato printing. You will need a big potato and a small one. Ask an adult to cut them for you. You can keep your potatoes in the refrigerator for a few days. Wash, dry and wrap them up first.

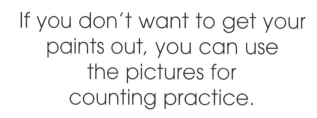

If you don't want to get your paints out, you can use the pictures for counting practice.

Potato printing

1. Lay some kitchen paper towels onto a thick pile of newspaper.

2. Pour paint on top. Spread out with the back of a spoon.

3. Cut a potato in half. If you like you can make a handle by cutting it like this.

4. Lay your printing paper onto another pile of newspaper.

5. Press the potato in the paint. Then press it onto the printing paper.

6. You can print two or three times before putting more paint on.

I can count to 1

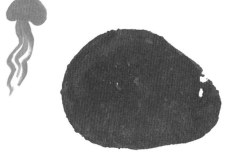

1. Print a body with a big potato.

2. Add a tail with a brush.

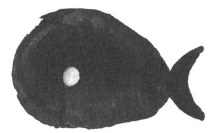

3. Finger paint a white eye.

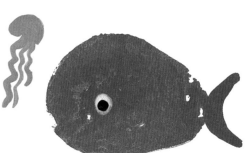

4. When dry, add a black middle to the eye.

5. Paint a big mouth with a brush.

6. Finger paint a waterspout.

1 whale

I can count to 2

1. Print a black body with a big potato. Leave to dry.

2. Print a white tummy with a smaller potato.

3. Add a yellow beak with a brush.

4. Paint 2 black flippers.

5. Paint 2 orange feet.

6. Paint a white and black eye.

2 penguins

I can count to 3

1. Print a body with a big potato.

2. Print a head with a small potato.

3. Paint a beak and an eye.

4. Paint 3 head feathers and 3 tail feathers.

5. Paint some legs with a brush.

6. Add 3 toes to each leg.

3 birds

I can count to 4

1. Print a body. Print eyes on top with your finger.

2. Paint **4** legs with a brush.

3. Paint some toes on each leg.

4. Print white spots in the eyes with your finger.

5. Print black dots in the eyes. Paint a mouth with a brush.

6. Use your finger to print **4** spots on the tummy.

4 frogs

I can count to 5

Flowers

1. Print a flower middle with your finger.

2. Print **5** petals with a small potato.

3. Paint a stalk with a brush.

Bees

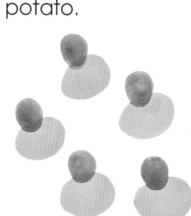 

1. Print **5** bee bodies with your finger.

2. Finger paint wings on the bees.

3. Paint black stripes with a brush.

5 flowers

I can count to 6

1. Print a cat's face with a potato. Add ears with a finger or brush.

2. Print white eyes with dark dots. Use your finger.

3. Paint a black nose with a brush.

Mice

4. Add a mouth, and 6 whiskers.

1. Print 6 mice with your finger.

2. Finger paint an ear. Add tail, nose and eye.

6 cats

I can count to 7

1. Print a body with a big potato.

2. Print an eye with your finger.

3. Paint a tail and a fin with a brush.

4. Paint a mouth with a brush.

5. Paint **7** spines with a brush.

6. Print **7** spots with your finger.

7 fish

I can count to 8

1. Use a big potato to print a body.

2. Paint 2 stalks. Print eyes on top.

3. Print the middles with your finger.

4. Paint the mouth.

5. Paint 8 legs.

6. Put claws on the top legs.

8 crabs

I can count to 9

1. Print a small potato 3 times for a body.

2. Print a head. Finger paint a pointed tail.

3. Print eyes with your finger.

4. Print dots in the eyes. Paint a nose and a mouth.

5. Paint 9 legs. Put 3 on each part of the body.

6. Print 9 feet with your finger.

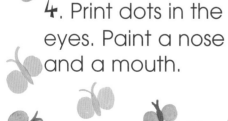

9 caterpillars

I can count to 10

1. Print a head with your fingertip.

2. Paint a body with your finger.

3. Print wings with a potato.

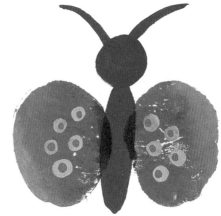

4. Paint 2 feelers with a brush.

5. Print 10 big spots with your finger - **5** on each wing.

6. Paint 10 dots inside the spots.

10 butterflies

I can count to 20

There are 20 ducks on these two pages. Can you count them all?

Now count how many ducks are swimming.

How many ducks have a yellow beak?

How many ducks have yellow feet?

How many ducks are pecking corn?

How many ducks have a worm?

See page **160** for how to paint ducks like these.

I can count to 30

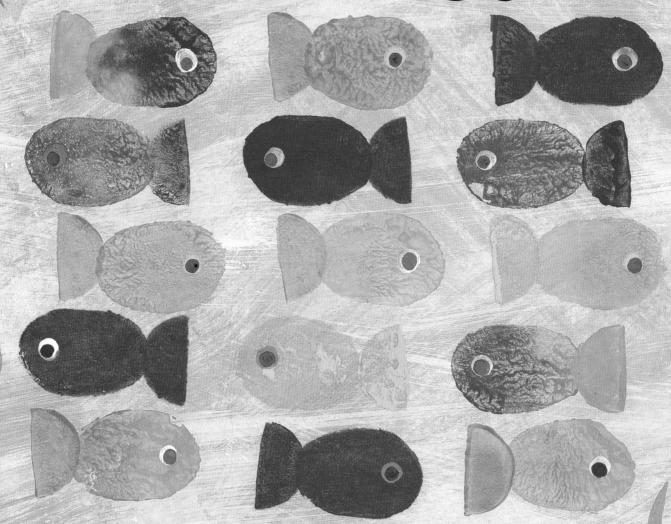

There are 30 fish on these two pages. Can you count them?

Now count how many of them have a green tail.

Find out how to print fish on page 160.

How many fish are swimming from left to right?
How many yellow fish are there?
How many fish have a yellow tail?

155

I can count to 40

There are 40 mice on these two pages. Can you count them?

Now count how many mice have a white tail.
How many pink mice are there?

Look back at page **142** to find out how to print mice.

How many mice have purple ears?
How many mice have pink ears?
How many mice have white ears?
How many mice have a piece of cheese?

I can count to 50

There are **50** spiders on these two pages. Can you count them all?

Now count how many black spiders there are.
How many spiders have pink legs?

Find out how to print spiders on page 160.

How many spiders have green eyes?
How many spiders have black legs?
How many spiders are green with yellow legs?
How many yellow spiders are there?

Duck, fish and spider

For a duck

1. Print a body with a quarter of a potato.

2. Use a small potato to print a head.

3. Paint a beak and 2 feet.

4. Add an eye with your finger.

For a fish

1. Print a body with a potato.

2. Print a tail with a quarter of a potato. Paint an eye.

For a spider

1. Print a body with a potato.

2. Paint 8 legs and 2 eyes.

I can add up

Adding	162	Spotty animal	178
Funny clowns	164	Snowman	180
Mice and cheese	166	In the garden	182
Pretty princesses	168	Penguin party	184
Bears and bees	170	Hungry turtles	186
Caterpillar's shoes	172	Wheels on the train	188
A castle and flags	174	Jolly juggler	190
Teeth and tentacles	176	Sheep in a field	192

Adding

This part of the book is full of activities which ask you to cut things out and add them to the pictures. Sometimes, you will have to take things away and count again. Cut the things out quickly, but carefully. Don't worry about how neat they are.

When you start to add up, point to each thing as you count it and say the number. Later, when you are good at adding up, you may not need to point to things as you count.

You may find it easiest to start counting from the left side of a page and move to the right.

How many butterflies have spots?
Cut some spots for the others. Put them on.
How many butterflies have spots now?

Funny clowns

How many clowns
have hats?
Cut out hats for
the other clowns.
How many hats
are there now?

How many blocks have spots?
Cut spots for the rest.
How many spots are there now?

Mice and cheese

How many mice have a tail?
How many mice have no tail?

Cut a piece of yarn.
Give it to the mouse with no tail.
How many tails are there now?

How many plates have cheese?
How many empty plates are there?

Cut some yellow paper.
Put a piece on each empty plate.
How many pieces of cheese are there now?

Pretty princesses

How many princesses have crowns?
Cut out a paper crown. Give it to the princess without one.
How many crowns are there now?

How many rings have jewels? Cut out jewels for the rest.
How many jewels are there now?

Bears and bees

How many bears are awake?
Draw and cut out open eyes
for the others.
Put them on the sleeping
bears.
How many are
awake now?

2 honey pots have lids.
Cut out lids for the others.
How many lids are there now?

Count the bees on the
other page.
Add on the bees on this page.
How many bees altogether?

Caterpillar's shoes

Count the butterflies on this page.
Add on the ones on the other page.
How many altogether?

4 flowers have leaves.
Cut a leaf for the
other flower.
How many now?

How many shoes is the
caterpillar wearing?
How many legs have
no shoes?

Cut shoes from paper
and put them on his
legs.
How many shoes are
there now?

A castle and flags

How many windows
are in the castle?
Cut 3 more from
paper and put them
on the castle.
How many windows
are there now?

How many flagpoles
have flags?
Cut out 2 more and
put them on empty
flagpoles.
How many flags are
there now?

How many rocks?
Add 1 more.
How many rocks
are there now?

Teeth and tentacles

How many teeth does the big fish have?
Give him **3** paper teeth.
How many teeth are
there now?

How many shells
have pearls inside?
Make foil pearls for the others.
How many pearls are there now?

How many tentacles
does the octopus have?
Cut **2** more from yarn.
How many now?

177

Spotty animal

How many nests
have eggs?
Cut out **3** more eggs.
How many eggs are
there now?

How many spots does
this animal have?
Cut out **5** more spots.
Put them on the
animal.
How many spots
are there now?

179

Snowman

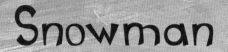

How many buttons does the
snowman have?
Cut 4 more from paper.
Put them on his tummy.
How many are there now?

How many birds
have a tail?
Cut paper tails for
the others.
How many tails are
there now?

Cut out **1** snowflake
from paper.
Add it to the others.
How many are there
altogether?

181

In the garden

How many flowers are on the bush?
Cut out **3** more flowers and
add them.
How many are there now?
Caterpillars eat **2** of the
flowers. Take them off.
How many flowers are left?

How many pots have a worm on top?
Cut more worms from yarn for the others.
How many worms are there now?

How many carrots
have leaves?
Cut out a paper leaf
for the one without.
How many carrots
have leaves now?

Penguin party

How many penguins
have fish?
Cut out **6** more and
give them to the
penguins.
How many fish are
there now?

Three penguins ate
their fish.
Take **3** fish away.
How many fish are
there now?

How many icebergs
are in the sea?
Add **2** more.
How many are
there now?

Hungry turtles

How many turtles have a
leaf to eat?
Cut out leaves and give
them to the others.
How many turtles are
eating now?

1 turtle finishes his
leaf.
Take 1 leaf away.
How many leaves
are left?

187

Wheels on the train

How many wheels does the train have?
Add buttons for the missing wheels.
How many wheels are there altogether?

How many packages are in the wagons?
Add 3 more. How many now?
One package falls out. Take 1 away. How many are there now?

Jolly juggler

How many shapes
are balancing below?
Cut out **4** more and
put them on top.
How many are
there now?
3 shapes topple off.
Take **3** away.
How many are left?

Count the red
clubs. How many
are there?
Count the blue
ones. How many
altogether?

This juggler is juggling 3 things. Cut 3 more things from a magazine and put them on. How many is he juggling now?

The juggler drops 2 things. Take 2 of them away. How many things are there now?

Sheep in a field

How many sheep are in the field?
How many more do you
need to make 10?
Use your fingers to
help you count.

How many more
flowers do you need
to make 10?
How many more
birds will make 10?

Fun with numbers

Number fun	194	Roly-poly puppies	210
Sailing boats	196	Four fat bears	212
Spiders' legs	198	Jumping frogs	214
Busy cranes	200	Spotted giraffes	216
Planes	202	Party cakes	218
Shy monkeys	204	Something fishy	220
Builders' trucks	206	Busy bees	222
Greedy parrots	208	How many spots?	224

Number fun

This part of the book is full of different activities, such as the one below, which involve counting, adding, taking away or sharing. Some of the pages ask you to cut paper shapes to help you to count. You don't need to worry about how neat they are.

Going shopping

How many things are in this basket?

Cut pictures of any kind of food
from a magazine or newspaper.

Put the
pictures in
this empty
basket so
that both
baskets
contain the
same number
of things.

Sailing boats

How many boats are there altogether?

How many boats have **2** sails?

Cut sails from paper and put them on the boats so that each one has **2** sails.

How many sails are there now?

Spiders' Legs

How many spiders
are there
altogether?

How many legs
does each spider
have?

Which spider has
the most legs?

Cut some pieces of
yarn for legs. Put
them on the spiders
so that each one
has **8** legs.

199

Busy cranes

How many boxes is each crane lifting?
How many boxes are the cranes
lifting altogether?

Cut some boxes from paper.
Add 1 box to each crane.
How many boxes are there
altogether now?

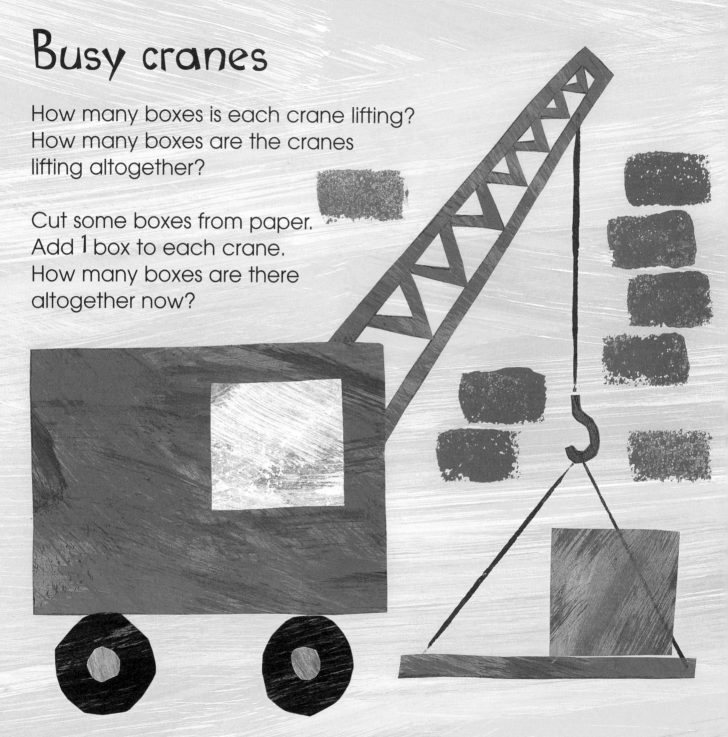

Add another box to
each crane.
How many boxes are
the cranes lifting now?

Planes

How many planes can you see?

Cut clouds from paper and cover **3** planes. How many planes can you see now?

Cover **2** more planes with paper clouds. How many planes are left?

Shy monkeys

How many monkeys
are in the tree?

Cut big leaves from
paper and put them
over the small monkeys
to hide them.

How many monkeys
are left?

Hold up 1 finger for
each monkey that
is left.

One monkey goes
looking for food.
Put 1 finger down.
How many monkeys
are left now?

Builders' trucks

Cut out some bricks from paper. Put 3 bricks on the back of each truck.

Draw a circle with your finger around each group of 3 bricks.

How many groups of 3 are there?

Count all the bricks. How many bricks are there altogether?

Now do the same thing with 2 bricks on each truck.

207

Greedy parrots

Use pieces of pasta as treats for the parrots.

Guess how many treats you will need, for each parrot to have 1 treat.
Give each parrot 1 treat to see if you were correct.

Give each parrot 2 treats.
How many treats are there altogether?

Give each parrot 3 treats.
How many are there now?

Roly-poly puppies

Cut **2** plastic straws into **12** pieces to make pretend bones.

Share the bones between the puppies until they have all been used up.

Share all the bones between **2** puppies. How many bones does each one have?

Try sharing all the bones between **3** puppies. How many does each one have now?

Four fat bears

Squeeze small
pieces of kitchen
foil to make 10 little
fish shapes.

Give each bear
2 fish.
How many fish are
left over?

How many bears
can have **3** fish
each?
How many fish are
left over?

How many bears
can have **4** fish
each?

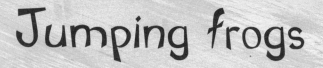

Jumping frogs

Make a frog like this.

Fold some paper.

Make two snips.

Fold back the paper between the snips.

Draw on a face and some front legs.

Put your frog on the big lily pad.

Make your frog jump on each pink lily until it gets to the reeds. How many jumps does it make?

How many jumps
does your frog make
if it goes on the
yellow lilies instead?

Spotted giraffes

Count the spots on the big giraffe. Then count the spots on the baby giraffe. Which has more spots?

Cut **5** spots from paper and put them on the baby. Which giraffe has more spots now? Which has the least spots?

Add a different
number of spots
to the baby.
Which has more
spots now?

Party cakes

How many plates have **6** cakes on them?

Cut out shapes from paper to make cakes. Put them on the plates so that all the plates have **6** cakes.

How many cakes did you add to the white plate to make **6**?
How many did you add to the blue plate?
How many did you add to the yellow plate?

Something fishy

Cut small shapes from paper, about the size of the spots on the fish.

Cover each spot on the orange fish below, with a paper shape. How many shapes did you need?

Cover the spots on the other fish. How many shapes did you need each time?

Look at the patterns of the spots on the fish.

Make a pattern with **4** paper shapes on the fish with no spots.

221

Busy bees

Draw 3 small bees and cut them out. Put 1 on each big flower.
Cut out 9 small squares.
Draw pink spots on 3 squares, blue spots on 3 and purple spots on 3.

Put the squares into a bag, then pull one out. If it's pink, move the bee on the pink flower along one.
If it's purple, move the bee on the purple flower, and so on.

Put the square back into the bag. Have lots more turns.

Which bee reaches the beehive first?
Which is second?
Which bee came third?

How many spots?

Count the spots in each picture.

Fold some kitchen foil around a piece
of cardboard, for a mirror. Stand
it along the straight edge
of each picture so you
can see its other half.
Count again. How
many spots does each
creature have now?